To _Shirley_ ,

because you're often in my prayers
and always in my thoughts.

From _Sue Thompson_

ISBN 1-56218-014-2

# Prayers for Today

Written by
Carolyn Herrmann

Good morning, Lord,
it's a lovely day—
so much like yesterday
and tomorrow
and yet so different.
Before I'm off and running,
I want to thank You
for the beautiful world
You created,
and for giving me life
to enjoy it.
I want to live each moment,
not looking back, nor ahead,
but remembering
something wonderful can happen
right now.

Give me wisdom, Lord,
as I go through this day.
The minutes and hours fly by,
and there are so many
decisions to make—
some thought out,
and some so quick,
there's no time to think.
I need Your wisdom guiding me,
even when I'm not aware of it.
Help me to do Your will
in all things.

Lord, I have too much to do,
      but it's all important.
Help me to set priorities
      so that I don't feel lost
            in the pace and the pressure.
Give me the wisdom and energy
      to accomplish what's necessary
            without wasting time or efforts
And help me make
            the best use of my day,
      remembering that time
                  is a precious gift
                  from You.

Lord, I want to spend
my coffee break with you...
You already know what's on my mind
and in my heart,
so I know
I don't have to impress You.
I can just relax and be myself.
And when I go back to work,
I know I'll really feel refreshed,
because You give me insight,
understanding, and direction.
Being with You
makes a coffee break
something very special.

*Lord*, help me be kind.
   *Don't* let me be so absorbed
         in my thoughts and plans
   that *I* rush through the day
            unaware of others.
*Help* me remember that people
            are more important
         than my list of things to do.
*Remind* me, *Lord*,
      to have time for others
            just as *You* always
            have time for me.

*Lord,*
        *every now and then I think*
*I have to do everything myself*
                *or else it won't get done.*
*I need to learn that my way*
                *is not the only way,*
*and that it's silly*
        *to worry about things*
                *that are beyond my control.*
*Remind me that I'm just me,*
                *and I'm important—*
        *but so is everyone else.*
*And together,*
        *we can all accomplish*
                *much more*
        *than any of us could alone.*

Help me to remember, Lord,
that, like the seasons of the year,
life brings continuous growth
and changes.
As long as I remember that,
I can look with expectancy
to all that lies ahead.
I can rest in the assurance
that You are in control
of the seasons of my life,
and everything that happens
is for my good and my growth.

When a lot of time goes by
        and I don't seem to accomplish
anything big or important,
                thanks, Lord,
for reminding me
        that life's successes
            are made up of little things.
            Lots of little flowers
make a beautiful bouquet.
When I remember that,
        I can have
        a sense of accomplishment
just by giving all the little things
            my best effort.

I'm happy, Lord!
   I'm always asking Your help
and sharing my problems
   with You, but right now,
   I want You to know
      I'm feeling happy.
   And I want to share
   the good times
      with You, too.

Good night, Lord.
It's been a pretty good day.
I'm encouraged
by the things that went well,
and challenged
by the things I can improve.
But, most of all, Lord,
I'm looking forward to tomorrow,
because I know
You'll be with me,
and whatever tomorrow brings,
we can handle it together.